FEAR NOT

A 33-Day Devotional Journey to Commemorate Each Year of Christ's Life on Earth… and to help readers facing cancer and other fears

By Anne Baxter Campbell

Foreword by Kathi Macias

From God's heart and mine to yours

Anne

Elk Lake Publishing
Fear Not

Copyright © 2014 by Elk Lake Publishing
Requests for information should be addressed to:
Elk Lake Publishing, Atlanta, GA 30024
ISBN-13: 978-1502981431
ISBN-10: 1502981432
All rights reserved. No part of this publication, either text or image may be used for any purpose other than personal use. Therefore, reproduction, modification, storage in a retrieval system or retransmission, in any form or by any means, electronic, mechanical or otherwise, for reasons other than personal use, - except for brief quotations for reviews or articles and promotions, is strictly prohibited without prior written permission by the publisher.

Cover Design: Kathryn Coffey

Unless otherwise indicated, Scripture quotations in this publication are taken from the Authorized King James Version of the Bible. Used by permission.

 Also quoted:

New King James Version, Holy Bible. Copyright c 1979, 1980, 1982 by Thomas Nelson, Inc., Publishers. Used by permission.

Scriptures taken from the Holy Bible, New International Version®, NIV®. Copyright © 1973, 1978, 1984, 2011 by Biblica, Inc.™ Used by permission of Zondervan. All rights reserved worldwide. www.zondervan.com The "NIV" and "New International Version" are trademarks registered in the United States Patent and Trademark Office by Biblica, Inc.™

All author royalties from the proceeds of this book will go to the National Cancer Society.

Elk Lake
PUBLISHING™

Dedication

This devotional is inspired by God and His courageous children who maintain an attitude of gratitude and grace through the most challenging circumstances imaginable. Perhaps the person who most greatly impressed me with this amazing courage is author Diann Hunt, who lost the battle but won the war. She graduated to heaven in November of 2013, one more victim of that ugly enemy, cancer. Diann's messages to her friends and family remained positive and filled with faith and love. My kudos also to her loving family, who obviously made her last days on this earth as pleasant as humanly possible. Her praise of them and of her God was constant and tender.

Not everyone lives through the challenges we all face, and sooner or later each of us will leave this earth and our family and friends. But—praise God—we do live through most of them!

May we follow Diann's example. May we grow closer to our Creator and Lord through every trial. May we exhibit grace to the final hour. And while we are able, may we fight to the last breath to overcome the enemies (diseases) and giants (catastrophes) that we all face in this life.

Acknowledgments

Thank You, Lord, for Your help in putting together this devotional. Thank You for all the willing writers who provided glimpses into their private lives in order to help the readers of this book. Thank You for the families who sacrificed so much to help and encourage. Thank You for medical staff who continually dedicate their lives to giving assistance and expertise to patients who aren't always sweet-natured and long-suffering. Thank You for medical research that gives us new understanding and hope for cures. And thank You for the readers herein; may they come closer to You, dear Lord, and realize how very much You love them. Amen.

Thank you also to the writers who contributed pieces for this devotional. I was so very enriched by the stories they shared, and I hope all the readers will be too.

God bless you all, writers and readers alike.

Foreword

I remember the first time I heard the term "cancer" applied to me. I was scarcely nineteen years old, with a seven-month old son at home. I had learned just weeks earlier that I was expecting my second child, and now, as I sat next to my husband, across the desk from the doctor who looked at us with a serious expression, I learned I also had a deadly disease.

We sat in his office, discussing the situation for at least fifteen or twenty minutes after that, but I don't remember a word that was said. After the word "cancer," I checked out. It wasn't until later, when we returned home, that my husband told me the doctor suggested I have an abortion, as I probably wouldn't be able to get through another pregnancy and deliver a healthy child.

Thankfully, though my husband and I weren't practicing Christians at the time, we prayed and believed we were not supposed to abort our child. This required that I spend the majority of that pregnancy in bed, plus have surgery mid-way through the pregnancy. None of this was easy, particularly with a little one who was just learning to walk and needed constant attention.

But with the help of friends and a faithful God, we got through it. I have now been cancer-free for forty-five years, and our second son—who was never supposed to be born healthy and strong—is a strapping six-footer who works in law enforcement.

God is amazing. My husband and I have since come to know Him on a personal basis, and we wish we'd had that sort of relationship when we went through the fires of cancer-related issues. A book like this would have been a huge help to both of us. For that reason, I happily and gratefully write this foreword and endorse this devotional. May it encourage and bless many, whether facing the fears of cancer or other such fears common to life. Let Him hold your hand and walk beside you—and when you haven't the strength to walk, lift your arms and allow Him to pick you up and carry you.

Kathi Macias (www.kathimacias.com) is the multi-award-winning author of more than 40 books, including *The 40-Day Devotional Challenge* and *The Singing Quilt*. A wife, mother, grandmother, and great-grandmother, Kathi "Easy Writer" Macias lives in Southern California with her husband, Al.

*Kathi Macias (www.kathimacias.com)

Prologue

Fear Not; neither be afraid.

In the Bible, God tells us over and over not to be afraid, that He is with us. Over the next thirty-three days, we'll explore stories and events where people had good cause to be afraid. Most of us have had times when we felt panicky. Yet God always says, "Do not be afraid." Yet how can we not be scared when we are facing the most fearful things in life?

Before you read each day's devotional, please read the accompanying scripture and then pray, asking God to show you what you need to see. Finally, read the devotional and write what comes to your heart. Trust that God will speak to you; He will.

My prayer is that before you come to the last word in this devotional, you will know Him better, trust Him more, and receive a small glimmer of just how immensely He loves you. He wants to walk with you through everything, good and bad, if you will just let Him.

Day 1

But now, thus says the Lord, who created you, O Jacob, And He who formed you, O Israel: "Fear not, for I have redeemed you; I have called you by your name; You are Mine."
Isaiah 43:1, NKJV

    In November of 2012, I was diagnosed with Stage IV aggressive breast cancer, which had spread to my chest wall, lung cavity, ribs, and spine. The pain nearly paralyzed me, but the fear-factor trumped all physical pain. What would happen to me? How long did I have to live? With a friend, I faced my diagnosis calmly, praying that God would soothe my pulsating heart. God answered prayers almost immediately by placing me in a weekly clinical trial three hours away, which would last three months. He also provided local friends with whom I could stay.

    Prayers around the world came to my rescue. After three months of treatment, my scans showed a nearly complete response to the infusion of drugs. No more lung fluid, abnormal lymph nodes, or bone disintegration. While I must continue to get treated indefinitely every three weeks, I know that God in His mercy has intervened and given me more months, if not years, to live. What a compassionate God we serve! I'm forever grateful to know Him.

Prayer: Lord, I don't know how to face the fear I feel. I want to hope, but I'm even afraid of that. Sometimes my heart feels like a cold, hard lump of lead. I am sometimes paralyzed, but I am paralyzed at Your feet. This is the only thing I can pray:

_____
_____
_____
_____.

Thank You, Lord, for hearing my heart's worst fears. Amen.

*Jan Baird Hasak, California

Day 2

After these things the word of the Lord came to Abram in a vision, saying, "Do not be afraid, Abram. I am your shield, your exceedingly great reward." **Genesis 15:1, NKJV**

Abram left home and family to travel to a place he didn't know. That had to be a fearful experience, not only for him but also for his wife and everyone else traveling with him. And yet they went because Abram was certain God had told him to do so.

After a time, he returned from a campaign where he rescued his nephew and household from robbers. As a result of this campaign, Abram gained riches, and God said He would give him even more.

Abram and Sarai had no children. He thought he would have to leave all he had to a servant when he died—a treasured servant, but still a servant. He and Sarai longed for children, but they were old and not likely to have any born to them.

God knew they wanted children. He told Abram, "Do not be afraid." Then He told Abram and Sarai they would have a child of their own. Finally He told Abram, "Look now toward heaven and count the stars if you are able to number them.... So shall your descendants be" (Genesis 15:5, NKJV).

Do you understand that God knows the desires of your heart, and that sometimes He must nudge you past your fears in order for those desires to be realized?

Many years ago, my husband and I had tried unsuccessfully to have children and were told by the doctor it was extremely unlikely we could. My tendency to miscarry, coupled with my husband's very low sperm count, added up to no more children. Yet we did have more—two sons to add to the daughter we already had (mine by a former marriage, his by adoption).

Do you know God loves you? Enough to give you all you need, regardless of your fears or doubts? Not all you want, maybe, but all you need. As you draw closer to Him, His desires become yours too, and then He is pleased to give you the desires of your heart.

Prayer: Dear Lord, may what You want be what I want. May the desires of my heart be so in tune with Yours that I will be unafraid to ask, and may I remain grateful even when You say no or give me only the things I truly need—even if they are not the things I asked for. Lord,

this is what I believe I need:

_____
_____
_____
_____ .

**Lord, let Your will be done.
No matter what, I give You my praise. Amen.**

*Anne Baxter Campbell, California

Day 3

And, behold, a woman, which was diseased with an issue of blood twelve years, came behind him, and touched the hem of his garment: For she said within herself, If I may but touch his garment, I shall be whole. But Jesus turned him about, and when he saw her, he said, Daughter, be of good comfort; thy faith hath made thee whole. And the woman was made whole from that hour.
Matthew 9: 20-22

The woman made a decision. For twelve years she had been in misery. She suffered from a bleeding condition that had placed her at the fringes of Jewish society for over a decade. In her culture, any woman who was bleeding was considered unclean.

Unclean women were to be shunned. Anyone who had contact with such a woman would automatically become unclean as well. So she stayed away from friends, family, and loved ones. Hers was a lonely life...no hugs or kisses, no caresses from a husband, no touch...ever.

One day she learned that Jesus would be passing through her town. She had heard of Jesus. She believed He was a Healer. She also believed Jesus was who He said He was and that He would do for her what He had done for so many.

But there were all those people...people who knew about her condition. She would have to make her way through the crowd to get to Jesus. What if she got caught? What would the Jewish authorities do to her?

The woman had to decide between fear and faith. She said to herself, "If only I may touch His garment, I shall be made well" (NKJV). She chose faith. Making her way to Jesus, she touched His cloak. Jesus turned and saw her. "Be of good cheer, daughter; your faith has made you well" (NKJV).

Prayer: Dear Loving and Caring Father, today I give my fears to you and receive faith. Specifically, I give you these fears and ask you to take them from me:____ _____. Today and every day I will trust in You, Father. Thank you for helping us to *fear not*. Amen.

*Marty Simons, Florida

Day 4

Then she went and sat down across from him at a distance of about a bowshot; for she said to herself, "Let me not see the death of the boy." So she sat opposite him, and lifted her voice and wept. And God heard the voice of the lad. Then the angel of God called to Hagar out of heaven, and said to her, "What ails you, Hagar? Fear not, for God has heard the voice of the lad where he is."
Genesis 21:16-17, NKJV

A couple of years after the birth of Isaac, Sarah became angry with her husband's son by her servant, Hagar. During the feast they had when she weaned Isaac, Ishmael had scoffed at his younger brother. Sarah banished both Hagar and her son. Abraham gave them a skin of water and some bread, and he sent them away with a heavy heart.

In the dry wilderness, Hagar and Ishmael ran out of food and water. She placed her son under a shrub and went a short distance from him, probably out of eyesight and hearing. She cried. She didn't want to watch her son die.

God told her not to be afraid because He had heard her son's voice. He knew where they were.

Have you been afraid for your children? There's nothing quite so frightening as wondering if your child will survive an illness or injury or if they will be found when they are lost. It's probably more frightening to the parent than it is to the child.

After they lost their first child to an unknown illness, my parents were afraid to let their next child experience anything. Every cry was a cause for paralyzing fear. Every nap found them hovering over him, making sure he still breathed. A roll off the couch brought panic.

Be assured that God hears the voice of your child. He hears your voice, too.

Prayer: Dear Father of fathers and mothers, hear me when I cry out to you. I ache with my children when they hurt, and I know You do, too. I ask You:_____.
I know You know how I feel, Lord. You watched Your own Son dying. Amen.

*Anne Baxter Campbell, California

Day 5

"Have I not commanded you? Be strong and of good courage; do not be afraid, nor be dismayed, for the LORD YOUR GOD is with you wherever you go."

Joshua 1:9, NKJV

When God passed the leadership baton to Joshua after Moses died, He said to him, "Be strong and courageous. Do not be afraid; do not be discouraged, for the Lord your God will be with you wherever you go." Joshua needed this personal confirmation of God's presence as he led the children of Israel across the Jordan River and into the Promised Land.

My two-year-old grandson, Gabriel, reinforced this truth to me in a humorous way. He'd been learning the verse for quite some time. One day when his mother had to discipline him, he clenched his fists, screwed up his face, and with eyes shut tight said, "Be strong and courageous!"

Like Gabriel, I've faced situations that provoke fear. Perhaps you have, too. Whether it's physical pain or a leadership challenge we dread, the Lord can take scripture we've memorized and whisper its truth into our ears: *Be strong and courageous. Do not be afraid.*

Prayer: Dear Father, you know that today I:_____
_____
_____.**Please help me to be strong and courageous, knowing that You will be with me wherever I go and in whatever I have to face. I know I can trust You, Lord, because You are my strength. Amen.**

*Eileen Rife, Virginia

**Adapted from Eileen Rife's devotional in Wit & Wisdom from the Wee Ones (Oak Tara, 2014), used by permission.

Day 6

And the LORD appeared to him the same night and said, "I am the God of your father Abraham; do not fear, for I am with you. I will bless you and multiply your descendants for My servant Abraham's sake."

Genesis 26:24, NKJV

Isaac had just arrived in Beersheba. That night, the Lord appeared to Isaac and reassured him that God would be with him. What inspired this encouragement?

Isaac had a lot of possessions. With a lot of possessions often comes a lot of concern. Isaac no doubt worried about water for his herds, especially since Abimelech's men had chased Isaac's shepherds away from two wells that Isaac's servants had dug. Probably he felt the weight of responsibility of providing for family and servants. Perhaps he tended to be a worrier. Or maybe God was preparing him for the confrontation he would have with a former adversary. Sometimes God does that—He tells us everything will be okay even before we know there is a problem. When we see the problem, we can understand and give thanks for His reassurance.

One time when my daughter was a teenager, she pleaded to spend the following school year with her father, a man who behaved with immaturity too many times for my comfort, including times when he would drop out of sight for months or even years. I told my daughter I would ask God for guidance. The only answer I got from God was, "Don't worry; it won't be a problem." Shortly before school would have started in the city where her father lived, we received a call from his new wife. He had disappeared, just as he had done when my daughter was a baby. He resurfaced a couple of years later, but the question of her spending a school year with him never arose again.

Prayer: Lord, please help me remember You know the future as well as You know the past. Help me trust, Lord, when uncertainties surround me. This is my request today, Lord:_____. Thank You, Lord, for knowing the answers before we even ask the question. Amen.

*Anne Baxter Campbell, California

Day 7

But as they sailed He fell asleep. And a windstorm came down on the lake, and they were filling with water, and were in jeopardy. And they came to Him and awoke Him, saying, "Master, Master, we are perishing!" Then He arose and rebuked the wind and the raging of the water. And they ceased, and there was a calm.

Luke 8:23-24, NKJV

From the first moment I heard the words "You have cancer," I have had moments or even days when fear washes over me. Even though it has been over five years, the fear that cancer will return raises its ugly head. Most often it occurs a few weeks before my scheduled appointment with the oncologist. Other times it's when I sense or experience something different in any part of my body.

In Luke 8:22-26, we read that Jesus and His disciples were in a boat when a sudden storm came up while they made their way across the lake. The disciples feared for their lives as the wind blew hard and the waves rose high, tossing and turning their boat. "Master, Master, we are perishing!" they cried. Jesus ordered the storm to calm. He then turned to the men and asked them where their faith was.

When I faced the storm called cancer, I needed to cope with the tools God had given me to face other challenges in my life. I prayed; I did meditation, allowing my body, mind, and soul to go deep into God's presence; through imagery, I visualized my body and mind in peaceful and healthy states.

God gave me the gift of writing, which I find helpful, relaxing, and rewarding, to express anger, fear, joy, or any other emotion. During those first years of surgery, tests, and chemotherapy, such words as storms, rain, lightening, and thunder were written in my journal. I believe my talents and strengths are God's gifts to me; it is what I do with them that are my gifts to God. My faith in God was and continues to be my beam of light, guiding me through times of fear.

**Prayer: Heavenly Father, I ask for Your help to hear Your words of encouragement, lean upon Your shoulders, feel Your comforting arms around me, and feel Your hands wipe away my tears. Lord, this is the encouragement I need from You:_____.
I know You are here to bring me through it. Amen.**

*Karen Ingalls, Florida

Notes:

Day 8

Now therefore be not grieved, nor angry with yourselves, that ye sold me hither: for God did send me before you to preserve life.
Genesis 45:5

Years before, Joseph's half-brothers sold him into slavery to an Egyptian caravan, and now he governed all of Egypt. Now, when his brothers came face-to-face with him, they didn't recognize him. He'd been a young man then, beardless and helpless against ten full-grown men. Now he dressed in Egyptian royal robes, probably had a beard in the current Egyptian style, and spoke to them through an interpreter.

They came to him during a great famine, asking to buy grain, and he accused them of being spies. He imprisoned one of his brothers and sent the rest home with the price of the food in their bags. Their fear that he would accuse them of thievery and throw them all in prison kept them from going back until they knew they would starve if they didn't. Even the thought of Simeon in prison didn't inspire them.

Worse, Joseph demanded they bring their youngest brother, Benjamin, if they ever came back or Simeon would die. They knew they must, but their fear was nearly more than they could stand. If this Egyptian governor kept Benjamin or imprisoned all of them, it would kill their father.

When Joseph finally revealed who he was to them, their first reaction was sheer panic. What if he chose to get even with them? Instead, Joseph told them not to feel badly about having sold him into slavery because God had allowed it to happen in order for Joseph to later be in a position to save lives during the famine.

Did you ever fear just punishment? You knew you had it coming, yet you received grace instead. God is like that.

Prayer: Lord, I know I fail to meet up to Your values, yet over and over You forgive me. I will not fear Your love. Please hear and forgive me when I ask Your pardon for: _____.Thank you for Your forgiving grace. Amen

*Anne Baxter Campbell, California

Day 9

They will have no fear of bad news; their hearts are steadfast, trusting in the LORD.

Psalm 112:7, NIV

Does your mind suddenly go to doom and gloom when you receive an adverse report?

My father is a corporate pilot. Flying airplanes has been his passion for as long as I can remember, and he's good at it. Being a pilot, he is required to have a physical each year. He has never had any serious medical problems; in fact, he was often told he was as healthy as someone much younger than his age.

He was once required to go for a medical test, which the doctor refused to do because he heard some irregular heart rhythms. When my father went to have it checked out, it was discovered he had heart blockages of over 90 percent. We were all shocked that nothing had been detected earlier. He was immediately scheduled for bypass surgery.

Naturally, I began to pray for my father's surgery to be a success and his recovery to be speedy. I could have fallen apart. With the severity of his blockages, I could have cried out to God in anger or even grief. But I learned it was possible to trust the Lord and not fear bad news.

We need not be afraid when bad news comes our way. God is in control. Though my father's heart surgery was a surprise to us, it didn't surprise God. Entrusting my father to God's care was the best place for him.

We can't walk around this life fearing bad news. The way we remove that fear is by fully trusting in God.

Do you fear bad news? Or do you trust God to handle any problem that comes your way?

Prayer: God, help me learn to trust You now so when bad news comes, I can face it without fear. You have proven You are trustworthy when:

_____

_____

_____. Help me to trust You when:_____

_____.

Thank You for being the God who is in control.

Amen. *Paula Mowery, Tennessee

17 Fear Not

Day 10

And he said, I am God, the God of thy father: fear not to go down into Egypt; for I will there make of thee a great nation.
Genesis 46:3

When Jacob's sons returned from Egypt with an abundance of food plus wagons to take their father back to Egypt with them, he didn't know what to think. Then they told him Joseph was alive and waiting for him, and the Bible says his heart stopped. I can imagine! The beloved son he'd thought torn to pieces by wild animals years earlier was alive and governing Egypt.

And now they wanted Jacob to move to Egypt, to leave home and friends behind and go to a far country. Even with the prospect of seeing his son again, I imagine he felt reluctance to move. He wasn't young any more.

When I was in my fifties, God asked me to move to California. California? You've got to be kidding me! The place in this land of ours I least wanted to live. Overcrowded cities and freeways, traffic jams, weird attitudes. *Not there, Lord!* Actually, I didn't want to move anywhere. I loved where I lived in Phoenix, Arizona. I owned a nice home and had literally put down roots, planting trees and bushes around the house.

Yet God called me to California with several confirmations. Did you know that if God calls you to California, you can't be obedient by staying in Arizona? With more reluctance and tears than you can imagine, I went—and felt guilty about crying over His direction.

Then I found people in the Bible who went reluctantly: Moses, Jonas—and even Jesus, when it came to the Cross. Yet each submitted to the Father's will and went. Remember the parable about the two sons (see Matthew 21:28-31)? The obedience is in the actual *going* to do His will, not in just the *saying* you will go.

Prayer: God, thank You that You go with me into the places that frighten me or sound implausible or impossible. Your love sustains me; Your courage strengthens and encourages me. Lord, this is my fearful place right now: _____.
Thank You for being the God even of my fearful places. Amen.

*Anne Baxter Campbell, California

Day 11

Even to your old age, I am He, and even to gray hairs I will carry you! I have made, and I will bear; Even I will carry, and will deliver you.
Isaiah 46:4, NKJV

    The third round of testing included even more mammograms and sonograms. I walked into a peaceful, dimly lit room. Soft, soothing music played while staff moved about quietly. I saw a number of women in green smocks similar to mine, some crying, most with worried faces. I realized I was not the only one this was happening to. I was grateful for a faith that did not leave me alone, a peace that whatever comes, God and I would handle this together.

    After three hours of preliminaries, the radiologist confirmed that an ultrasound-guided biopsy was needed. I experienced mild discomfort, but within fifteen minutes, it was over. The radiologist put a sympathetic hand on my shoulder. "There's one by the chest wall that's highly suspicious. But it's very small. You couldn't have found it any earlier."

    The nurse explained that in all probability I would only have to have a lumpectomy, but the doctor would probably order an MRI to be certain the lump was not invasive. The lymph nodes appeared clear.

    The next forty-eight hours were the worst as I waited for the doctor's confirmation. All the while, God reassured me with the verse He had given me earlier in the week from Isaiah: "Even to your old age, I am He, and even to gray hairs I will carry you!"

    "It is cancer," the doctor informed me. "You have the old-fashioned, garden-variety cancer. It is invasive, but we found it early."

    Though I did not know what the future would hold, I knew who held the future, just as I knew there was nothing that would come to me outside of God's permissive will. I am now in remission, and not a day throughout chemotherapy and radiation did God fail to send me hidden blessings, treasures within the mire. He's good like that.

Prayer: Thank you, Lord, for trials. These are the ones I now face:_____
_____. In these trials, Lord, I see You as never before. You are the Giver and the Sustainer, and all I need is in You. Amen.
*Linda Wood Rondeau, Florida

Day 12

I sought the LORD, and he heard me, and delivered me from all my fears.
Psalm 34:4

It was a day like any other, but one phone call shattered any semblance to the ordinary. Out of the blue, with no advance warning, my dad died. While recovering from routine surgery, complications arose suddenly; just as suddenly, he was gone.

Later, I remember waking in the middle of the night with one overwhelming sensation—fear. Fear so raw and terrible I could hardly breathe. Numb with grief and loss, dread and anxiety consumed my life. My two small children had just lost a grandmother a short time ago, and now this. Where was God at this heartbreaking moment?

This tragic event happened ten years ago, yet I still recall it with sharp vividness. The pain and grief, while muted, are still retrievable in my mind. Since then, additional trials, tempering, and unwanted growth have filled my life, and even now I don't understand why certain things happen. But I now know where God was then, and where He always is—right beside me. David said that he sought the Lord, and He delivered him from all his fear. The problem is, most of the time we don't seek the Lord. We seek other things instead. However, this world only provides temporary comfort and momentary hope. Our real refuge is in the arms of God, where fear is not and peace is always.

In life there is no shortage of things to fear. Our own death and the death of someone we love may be the biggest fears of all. When these loom large, there is one thing, one promise that is sure to bring lasting relief. Seek the Lord and He will deliver you. With such a promise, why would we want to seek anything else?

Father God, help me to seek You when I am overwhelmed with these fears: _____. Thank You for Your promise to deliver me. Coming from You, I know this promise can never be broken. Amen

*Chris Barratt, Michigan

Day 13

Then I said unto you, Dread not, neither be afraid of them. The Lord your God which goeth before you, he shall fight for you, according to all that he did for you in Egypt before your eyes.
Deuteronomy 1:29-30

Moses reminded the Israelites about the time they had become fearful to go where God said to go—where, in fact, they had refused to go. Have you ever refused to do what God wanted you to do?

Not all sins are blatant and ugly. Sin merely means missing God's target, not hitting the bull's-eye. Fear can stop us so easily. Fear of what people will think. Fear of losing a friend or antagonizing a foe. Fear of revenge. I have been there more times than I can count.

God's path is seldom easy, but it's the only one lit with His lamp. He might not always lead on the broad, level, flower-lined path. Nettles and thorns keep trying to creep in from every side. Birds of prey swoop over. Wolves howl. It can be fearful there.

God never promised an easy path, but He did promise to go with us. Every jab of a doctor's needle, every bruise from every fall, every paper cut He feels right along with you. He bleeds when you bleed, hurts when you hurt, cries when you cry. Don't be afraid to go where He says to go. Don't refuse for fear of what might happen.

Remember always that He loves you. He loves you just as though you were His only child. He won't ask you to do anything He wouldn't do Himself. He won't lead you anywhere that He won't be right beside you. He wouldn't ask you to do this thing if it weren't needed for your good, for someone else's, or for both. March forward with trust and without fear.

Prayer: Lord, I know You also had a path to walk that frightened You. I know You understand how I feel. Lord, on this day, this is why I'm afraid to go:

_____
_____
_____. **Thank You, Lord, for walking with me in the places that frighten me. Amen.**

*Anne Baxter Campbell, California

Day 14

I the LORD thy God will hold thy right hand, saying unto thee, Fear not; I will help thee.
Isaiah 41:13

Have you ever had to walk by faith? You know God is with you because His Word tells you He will never leave nor forsake you, but your feelings are so numb and raw you don't feel His presence. I've been there. Not for just a few days, but nearly a year.

The year after my fourteen-year-old son died, all that carried me through was my faith and belief that God was with me. I didn't feel God. I didn't hear His voice. I didn't even spend much time with Him. I was too busy drowning in grief. I was numb.

The devil would have loved to convince me that because I didn't feel God or spend time with Him, I was lost, even backslidden. But I knew this wasn't so. His words I had hidden in my heart over the years assured me He was there. He held my hand, carrying me through this time of bereavement.

What was the turning point? When did I begin to experience God again? I can't tell you a day or the hour that happened. What helped me was remembering the voice of my counselor whispering to me, "Be kind to yourself. Take care of yourself. God is there. He understands. His own Son died. He has felt this pain, too." Those very words are my mantra, my "go to" phrase whenever I feel grief overwhelming me.

Prayer: Dear God, we know Your plan is not for us to walk in fear. We can trust that You are our salvation. You hold our hands and help us on our journey. Be with each of us today and always. Amen. Tell God today how you trust Him to help you face your fears:

_____
_____
_____.

*Cindy Loven, Arkansas

Day 15

Behold, the Lord thy God hath set the land before thee: go up and possess it, as the Lord God of thy fathers hath said unto thee; fear not, neither be discouraged.
Deuteronomy 1:21

Moses reminded the Israelites of when their fathers had refused to go and possess the Promised Land because they thought there were giants in the area. Now he tells them God prepared the land for them and they don't have to worry about anything.

Have you ever been in a place where the giants seem bigger than the Promised Land? Are you there now?

Remember the story of Simon Peter getting out of the boat to walk to Jesus? As long as Peter kept his gaze on Jesus, he did a fine job of walking on water. Then he noticed the waves and the wind, and his focus changed. He fixated on the giants and would have drowned had Jesus not taken his hand.

You and I can find ourselves in the same boat—or out of the same boat. Afraid of the giants when we should be remembering the Lord knows how to conquer giants and waves and high winds.

We should also remember Jesus stands with His hand ready to catch us when we fall. There's another verse in Micah 7:8, which I love and find reassuring: "Do not rejoice over me, my enemy [the giants]; When I fall, I will arise; When I sit in darkness, The Lord will be a light to me" (NKJV). Notice that it doesn't say *if* I fall. The Lord knows we aren't always strong or constantly focused on Him. He knows we occasionally fall. But we will rise again. He will lift us out of the water. The Lord has said so.

Prayer: Lord, You know my weaknesses. You see me when I fall, and You reach Your hand out to lift me up again. These are the giants in my life that I can only overcome with your help:

_____

_____

_____. **Jesus, thank You for helping me back into the boat when I forget You're the Way to walk on water. Amen.**

*Anne Baxter Campbell, California

23 Fear Not

Day 16

"Are not two sparrows sold for a copper coin? And not one of them falls to the ground apart from your Father's will. But the very hairs of your head are all numbered. Do not fear therefore; you are of more value than many sparrows." **Matthew 10:29-31, NKJV**

It began as a "mom's day out." Joy Rose, my wife, went to see a movie before playing in the community band in Chico, CA. As she settled into the movie seat, a "weird" feeling turned into a seizure. She struggled out of the theater, collapsing in the hallway. Later, she woke up in the ambulance. In the emergency room, she was told she had a focal-point seizure. The seizure was caused by a golf ball-sized brain tumor above her right ear. Joy's tumor was diagnosed as *oligodendroglioma*.

The surgery in February 2009 at the University of California San Francisco Medical Center removed most of the tumor. It was an "awake" surgery, so she could respond as the surgeons probed the limit of tumor removal. The "rind" left behind was necessary to retain the use of the left side of her body. Following a year of chemotherapy, we moved to Minnesota.

In 2010 Joy began her follow-up care at the Mayo Clinic. In October 2011, a spot was identified in the same area as the original tumor. By December, the spot had grown to the size of a pea. In January 2012, surgery was done at the Mayo Clinic's Saint Mary's Hospital. The tumor had changed from a Grade 2 (slow growing and benign) to a Grade 3 (faster growing and malignant). She underwent six and a half weeks of radiation treatment and then chemotherapy treatment.

We relied on our church family heavily for prayer support throughout that time. They gave us strength, and the team approach to prayer was so helpful.

Prayer: Lord, fear can be debilitating, and fighting that off was and still is difficult. These are the fears I'm fighting now:

_____
_____.

Thank You, Lord, for the comforting arms and hands of people who pray. Amen.

*David Rose, Minnesota

24 Fear Not

Day 17

And the LORD said unto me, Fear him not: for I will deliver him, and all his people, and his land, into thy hand; and thou shalt do unto him as thou didst unto Sihon king of the Amorites, which dwelt at Heshbon.
Deuteronomy 3:2

When the nation of Israel began entering the Promised Land, King Og of Bashan came out against them. What was then Bashan is now called the Golan Heights. The meaning of the name Og is "gigantic." Apparently these were large people, and Israel had good cause to be fearful.

Many of us go through things that give us good cause to be fearful. Any sane person in the same circumstances would probably be afraid.

One night my teenage daughter was late coming home from a date. We lived in a small town, and I began driving around looking for her date's vehicle. I started out just being angry, but the longer I drove, the more fearful I became. I prayed and prayed and prayed. And then prayed some more.

When she got home well after midnight, she was shaking and crying, and the story came out. She and her then boyfriend had started chatting with a truck driver. Apparently the man had asked her if she'd ever ridden in a big rig before; she said she had not. He offered to take her for a ride. He took her for a ride, all right—and pulled over at the first wide spot in the road and began to assault her. Thank God, a policeman saw the truck parked in an unusual place and rescued her.

Any parent in their right mind would have been concerned. Any teenager in her right mind too. But God is bigger than a lecherous truck driver, bigger than dangerous situations, and bigger than our fears.

Prayer: Father, I'm so glad You are bigger than my fears and that You hear me when I call for help. This is what I need rescue from today:

_____
_____
_____
_____.

Thank You from the very depths of my being that You heed our prayers and rescue us. Amen.

*Anne Baxter Campbell, California

25 Fear Not

Day 18

For God has not given us a spirit of fear, but of power and of love and of a sound mind.**   **2 Timothy 1:7, NKJV

I was drowning in lies.

No, I wasn't lying to others; I was believing the lies being told to me. We know the devil comes to steal, kill, and destroy. And that's exactly what I was letting him do. He kept whispering in my ear:

"You're not good enough."

"You're a failure as a mother."

"Your husband despises you."

"You'll never succeed as a writer."

"God is not watching out for you."

I listened to each and every lie. I let them settle in my heart and fester in my soul. Life became a sucking pit of darkness, and I mourned the loss of the light.

Still, I soldiered on. I tried to pray. I studied the Bible. I hoped beyond hope that God would pull me out of this misery, that He would show me the way.

One morning, during Bible study with the girls, I introduced their new verse to memorize for the week: "Fear not, for I have redeemed you; I have called you by your name; You are Mine" (Isaiah 43:1a, NKJV). As I read those words, tears came to my eyes. The Creator of the Universe knew me. He called me by name. He knew exactly what I was going through and exactly who I was meant to be.

Fear is not from God. Doubt, failure, anger—these are not from God either. Satan feeds on our weaknesses; he renders us useless by making us feel inept. It is in these times that we need to call on Jesus, to ask for strength and wisdom to see through the lies.

Prayer: God, I know You will not leave me, but I have believed these lies: _____.
Please give me the discernment I need to break the shackles the devil uses to try to ensnare us. Amen.

*Ralene Burke, Kentucky

Day 19

If I take the wings of the morning, and dwell in the uttermost parts of the sea, even there Your hand shall lead me, and Your right hand shall hold me. **Psalm 139:9-10, NKJV**

God often reminds us in the Bible that He will lead us if we let Him. It seems like a repeated theme, doesn't it? How many reminders does it take for us to understand He is there, going before us, to lead us into the land He has for us? The Israelites weren't the only ones who couldn't (or wouldn't) see God's leading.

Sometimes we don't see His leading because we're looking in the other direction. Meanwhile, God is on the other side of us, whispering, "*This* way, not that way."

When I'm going His way, there is a greater peace. When I'm following Him, I like where I end up. When I'm on His path, the light sometimes is just enough to see the next step, so taking only that one small step is important. And if we don't see the next step? Stand still, expecting Him to show us when and where it is.

There was a time the Lord let me know a path He wanted me to walk. I stubbornly insisted on a different way, my own way. I chose the way of the party crowd and ignored His way. What resulted is years of heartache, not just for myself but also for so many others, especially members of my own family. I should have been afraid, but I strode forward boldly on that wrong path for years. I cringe when I think of the places I took Him—but still He brought me back.

Prayer: Lord, please keep showing me which way to go. I'm afraid of taking the wrong path again. Lord, is this the path You want me on?

_____
_____
_____
_____**. Lord, thank You for Your light on the right path. Let me never go blind again! Amen.**

*Anne Baxter Campbell, California

Day 20

Fear not, Paul; thou must be brought before Caesar.
Acts 27:24a

    I was about ten years old, walking home from school one day. As usual, my little brother, sister, and I stopped in at the small store on the corner opposite the one-room school house. The proprietors always welcomed the children coming in after school and always had a little bin full of free penny candy or some other treat for us.

    But this day I wanted something more, so I found my way to the *real* candy and slipped a Baby Ruth candy bar into my pocket. We had a quarter-mile walk ahead, so I dawdled behind my younger siblings and the others kids while I surreptitiously ate my stolen treat.

    Mothers are omniscient; they know everything. It wasn't long before Mom somehow knew about that Baby Ruth candy bar. (No doubt, someone tattled.) She promptly put me into the car and drove me back to that store where I confessed my theft and paid for it with a nickel out of my own precious piggy bank…all the while trembling with fear.

    In the verse above, the Apostle Paul was a prisoner on a storm-tossed ship bound for Rome. They feared sinking, but the Lord assured Paul he wasn't going to die because he had that appointment with Caesar (see Acts 27).

    I was a prisoner of my own sin, and my "Caesar" was that store owner whose trust I'd betrayed. God saw to it that I kept my "appointment."

Prayer: Heavenly Father, thank You for loving us even when we do wrong. Because of Your unconditional love, I know I don't need to fear confessing my sins to You because You always stand ready to forgive. These are the wrongs I have done that I ask You to forgive:

_____

_____. This child of Yours is grateful that with You, sins confessed are remembered no more. Amen.

*Peggy Blann Phifer, Wisconsin

Day 21

Say to them that are of a fearful heart, Be strong, fear not: behold, your God will come with vengeance, even God with a recompense; he will come and save you.   **Isaiah 35:4**

Before the American Civil War, one-fourth of the population of Ireland came to America, fleeing the potato famine that swept through their country. Just imagine the fear and anguish those desperate men, women, and children must have felt in leaving their friends, family, and homeland! Staying behind wasn't an option. More than one million people there died of starvation.

Most of us will never have to face such fear and dire circumstances. However, we all encounter trials. Sick children, lost jobs, personal illness, or the collapsed economy fill us with dread. Scared and alone, we wonder, "Does God really see me? Does He care? Where is He when the fabric of my life is being torn apart?"

Queen Esther felt the same way. She had every reason to believe her people, the Jews, would be slaughtered at the hands of the evil Prime Minister, Haman. The only way to save her countrymen was to put her own life in jeopardy. What makes Esther's story unique is her great faith and unyielding courage. She depended on God for everything.

Psalm 118:6 says, "The LORD is on my side; I will not fear: what can man do unto me?" Following these verses means trusting God and really believing He stands behind His word. God has promised that He will save us and care for us no matter the circumstances, whether they be famine, illness, or even death. Esther had to come to terms with this and face her fear head-on. She prayed, fasted, and then took God at His Word and stepped out in faith. What's stopping us from doing the same?

**Prayer: Lord, help me to believe what You say in Your Word. Increase my faith so when fears come, I can trust You for the outcome. I trust You with these fears: _____ _____.
You alone hold my life in Your hands. Amen.**

*Chris Barratt, Michigan

29 Fear Not

Day 22

"When you go out to battle against your enemies, and see horses and chariots and people more numerous than you, do not be afraid of them; for the Lord your God is with you, who brought you up from the land of Egypt." **Deuteronomy 20:1, NKJV**

    This is part of Moses's parting instructions to the priests. Moses knew his people would face what looked like insurmountable odds as they entered the Promised Land, and he knew they would be fearful. He told the priests they must encourage the Israelites and remind the people that their Lord and God would go with them to fight for them.

    There are times we need the reminder from someone that God will go before us to fight for us. If our battle is with illness, God goes before us. If we fight depression, God is there, standing between us and the enemy. If grief threatens to overwhelm us, God gives us His hand to lift us out of the deep morass. We can safely lean on His shoulder. We can depend on Him to fight when we feel too weak, too tired, too lacking in the proper weapons.

    When my youngest was a baby, he battled asthma constantly. He rattled each time he took a breath, and he was in and out of the hospital over and over. He was cranky and constantly wanted to be held. I couldn't fix a meal until his twelve-year-old sister or his father came home to walk the floor with him. In addition to being terrified I would lose him, I was exhausted and at the end of my rope. I didn't know what to do, nor did the doctors.

    Late one afternoon, we went to a prayer meeting. The man who stood in front of the room said to this crowd of about a hundred people, "One of you has a young child with something chronic. If you bring him forward, he will be healed." We did, and Ross was instantly healed of the asthma he'd had since a few weeks old. In addition, overnight he went from the crankiest to the happiest baby I'd ever seen. God sent the catalyst our one-year-old child needed for healing.

Prayer: Lord, thank You for being there through our battles against illness and weariness. Help us to remember You are there. This is my battle: _____.Thank You, God for the health of my child. Amen.

*Anne Baxter Campbell, California

Day 23

Serve the Lord with fear, and rejoice with trembling.
Psalm 2:11, NKJV

    I thought I was being followed. Being downtown in a strange city gave me a sense of unease. Two unpleasant-looking fellows seemed too interested in my sightseeing. A nearby cathedral was having a service, so I went inside. The two entered also, but I lost them in the building. Was my fear actual or imagined? I don't know. It was, however, a motivation to find a place of safety.

    Fear is natural to the heart. The issue is whether it motivates or paralyzes. It can be harnessed for good, or allowed to run riot and thereby cause ruin. When the Bible says, "Fear God," it means to be motivated to honor, serve, obey, and know Him. The sadness for some is they are petrified about meeting God, so they try to bribe, curse, or hide from Him.

    As I read the Bible I see we are wise to fear the Almighty. He is holy; we are not. He is Truth, while our lives are full of lies. He is Judge; we are guilty. However, our God is also Mercy and Grace. He is able to tie together all aspects of His Being with Love. It was His Love that dealt with all that caused us to be paralyzed at the thought of Him. The Cross is ever the answer to our fear. It is the reason for our devotion to our Savior and Lord. Such fear is healthy, life-giving, and motivational for worship and service.

Lord, many things in life give us cause to fear; please show us from Your Word Your answers to them. Motivate us by Your mercy to live in the wisdom that reverence for You produces. These are my good fears:

_____
_____
_____.

These are the ones that are not so good:

_____
_____
_____.

Please help me to remember the difference is in You. Amen.

*Ray N. Hawkins, Tasmania, Australia

Day 24

Be strong and of a good courage, fear not, nor be afraid of them: for the Lord thy God, He it is that does go with thee; He will not fail thee, nor forsake thee.
Deuteronomy 31:6

Moses told his people that God would go before them into the unknown. He would not depart from them. He would walk with them, scout out the dangers, and fight for them.

I was forty years old, time to begin the yearly mammograms. I checked myself for lumps before going in for a checkup, and I found three of them—big ones! When I saw the doctor, he told me I would need a biopsy and scheduled me with a surgeon.

My first reaction was cold, sweaty fear. Did I think about turning to God? Well, sorta. I was a Christian but not practicing my beliefs, and my fear was bigger than my faith. Besides, I hadn't exactly been living for Him lately. He had good reason to punish me, I knew. Instead, I was blessed—the lumps turned out to be liquid-filled, non-cancerous cysts that came and went periodically. I began breathing normally again, and gave thanks with many promises to become a better Christian.

Moses had the same problem with his people—their fear was bigger than their faith. Something I've learned, though, is that God is bigger than our fears.

Prayer: Lord, whenever I am fearful, I turn to You. Knowing You walk the same path with me helps. Knowing You walk not beside me but in front of me, between me and the unknown, leading the way, is a comfort. I know You will see dangers, stumbling stones, and thistles before I know they are there, and protect me from them. Hold my hand, Lord, when I am afraid. Father, these are the dangers I fear:

_____
_____
_____.You know what is best, and You know the road to healing and rest. Amen.

*Anne Baxter Campbell, California

32 Fear Not

Day 25

"Have I not commanded you? Be strong and of good courage; do not be afraid, nor be dismayed, for the Lord your God is with you wherever you go."   **Joshua 1:9, NKJV**

"Be strong and of good courage." Easier said than done, right? Especially when you've been given life-changing news. When diagnosed with cancer, I thought of every possible worst-case scenario, but I prayed for strength and courage. It wasn't until I trusted the Lord to make me strong that I was able to be courageous.

"Do not be afraid." How can you *not* be afraid after a cancer diagnosis? I was plagued by thoughts of invasive testing, intense treatment plans, pending surgeries, possible declining health. Would I be able to help my husband raise our beautiful daughters? Would I survive? I was terrified, though I continued to pray. I vividly remember the morning of my first chemotherapy treatment. After weeks of fear, I woke up with an indescribable sense of peace. The Lord had made me ready for the unknown.

"Nor be dismayed." It's easy to feel overwhelmed when faced with changes over which we have no control. I often felt my hands were tied throughout treatment. (How discouraging for a woman with admitted control issues!) The chemo made me sick and tired, and my body hurt horribly, but there was nothing I could do. I lost my hair, eyebrows, and eyelashes, but again, nothing could be done. Giving up control was one of hardest parts of my cancer. This lesson was a long time coming for me, but I finally learned that whenever I felt out of control and discouraged, I must give it all to God.

The Scriptures promise us that the Lord is with us wherever we go. It's normal to feel alone while fighting cancer. It's normal to feel that no one understands what we're going through. But we are not alone, and others do understand! During this most challenging part of my life, I learned to look for Him, lean on Him, and trust Him with everything. Never in my life have I felt the presence of the Lord as distinctly as I did through cancer.

Prayer: Lord, thank You for being in control. Please take these out-of-control issues from me:_____. I'm glad You are always with us wherever we go! Amen
***Amy Disney, Indiana**

Day 26

"Fear not, for I am with you; Be not dismayed, for I am your God. I will strengthen you, Yes, I will help you, I will uphold you with My righteous right hand." Isaiah 41:10, NKJV

When I was about ten years old, my friend Eugenie Fuller and I went for a hike on one of the hills that lie on the north edge of Challis, Idaho. Things went well until we had to cross the green rock.

The green rock is a series of greenish colored, solid though rather soft rock faces that lie on about a thirty-degree slope on the hill north of Challis. The rock is covered with fine sand and gravel.

Eugenie made it across without a problem. Even though she slid a little, she crabbed her way across the slope to the area where it would be safe to descend to the bottom of the hill where we could make our way home.

We had hiked these hills several dozen times before, but for some reason this time was different. Maybe it was the kitten that had followed us. I guess he was tired because he didn't want to follow us any farther. We couldn't carry him; we needed two hands, two feet, and ten-year-old bottoms to keep us from sliding over the cliff at the bottom of the green rock. We needed to leave the little guy behind and move forward.

I panicked. Each move I made slid me a little closer to the edge. My stomach turned into a lump of burning ice. I began to cry. Petrified with fear, I couldn't move.

If only I had known then what I know now—that God will help us over the scary parts—it wouldn't have taken Eugenie so long to talk me into moving to safety.

Prayer: Father, You are Master even of the slippery slopes. Thank You for holding my hand when I'm frightened and keeping me from sliding over the cliffs. These are the terrifying places I hand to You:

_____

_____

_____.Amen.

*Anne Baxter Campbell, California

34 Fear Not

Day 27

But the woman fearing and trembling, knowing what was done in her, came and fell down before him, and told him all the truth. And he said unto her, Daughter, thy faith hath made thee whole; go in peace, and be whole of thy plague. **Mark 5:33-34**

    The poor woman had spent all her money trying to find a cure for her twelve years of bleeding. Jesus was her only hope. She pushed her way through the crowd toward the Christ. *If I could touch the hem of His robe, I would be healed.* As soon as her fingers felt the edge of the Lord's garment, she was well.

    Jesus felt power leave Him and He turned around, asking who had touched His clothes.

    Humbled, the woman confessed.

    Jesus smiled. "Daughter, your faith has made you well" (NKJV).

    My husband's cancer was back—big time. We were nervous about his first appointment in oncology. I noticed a banner on the wall. It said "Best Oncology Clinic!" Patient signatures filled every imaginable space. I looked around. Everyone was upbeat and cheerful. My fears subsided; we were in the right place.

    The doctor prescribed the necessary treatment. We went to the pharmacy and were shocked that the medication ranged in the thousands of dollars. John and I walked to the car in silence. Finally, he said, "I'm not worth it."

    Tears welled up from my soul. I remembered a time in my life when my failure made me feel worthless. As God showed the woman with the bleeding issue that He cared for her, He showed me amazing love in the depth of my despair. I looked into John's eyes. "God loves you. We can take this to Him because He cares for you" (see 1 Peter 5:7).

    When I reminded John of that verse, he said, "I know. He has always taken care of me."

Prayer: Holy God, who was and is and is to come, thank You for Your great love. Thank You that we can cast our burdens on You. Here are my fearful burdens, Lord:_____.
Thank You for Your faithfulness. Amen.
*Sue Tornai, California

Day 28

The Lord is on my side; I will not fear. What can man do to me?
Psalm 118:6, NKJV

Not all fears are of physical danger.

I had made an innocent but hurtful statement about my husband's family. Not anything insulting and not a lie, but a written Christmas letter sent out to many people providing information his family didn't want shared. I hadn't intended harm or hurt by what I said, but it wound up causing a huge blowup in the family. You can chalk it up to growing up in different cultures, foot-in-mouth disease, or stark stupidity, but sometimes the things we say hurt deeply, even if that is not the intention.

After many apologies with not much response or forgiveness offered, the time had come to gather together to celebrate Christmas. I felt much the same as when I had been caught over that sliding green rock slope (see Day 26). I didn't know what would happen when we met for Christmas dinner. The very last thing in the world I would ever want to do is cause dissention in the family.

I literally spent hours in prayer about that day. I knew there was nothing more I could say or do to alleviate the situation, and I knew it would take an intervention by God Himself to relieve this fear and get us all past that uncomfortable laceration.

He did; the day went fine. No one brought up the subject again. Family hugs and kisses were passed around with never a knife wound inflicted.

Prayer: Father, You know me and how much I fear conflict, particularly within the family. Help me, Lord, to avoid even the innocent betrayal of trust. Grant that I would think and pray before speaking and especially before writing! I give these slips of the tongue and fingers to You and ask Your forgiveness:

_____

_____

_____. **Thank You, Lord, for all Your help and for Your abundant forgiveness. Amen**

*Anne Baxter Campbell, California

Day 29

"Peace I leave with you, My peace I give to you; not as the world gives do I give to you. Let not your heart be troubled, neither let it be afraid." **John 14:27, NKJV**

"Mom, it's cancer."

My daughter's uttering of the dreaded "C" word echoed in my mind long after I hung up the phone. I desperately wished she could avoid the pain and misery that lay ahead. Unfortunately, there's no way to bypass difficulty in this life. Suffering, pain, and even tragedy are all part of the human experience.

When we seek to do God's will and follow Him in all situations—blessed or tested—He offers peace and hope, even in the worst of times.

I was scared with every chemo treatment. The chemicals made her sick and caused her beautiful red hair to fall out. Nonetheless, we knew the drugs were necessary to kill cancer cells.

It's in times like these we're tempted to ask why. We might even begin to doubt God's love. Sadly, the more we question or try to cope with difficult situations in our own strength, the longer grief continues.

Peace isn't the lack of adversity, but rather the calm during life's storms. When guided by a master sailor, a sailboat can return safely to shore against the wind. More flowers grow in valleys than on mountaintops. God is with us in the stormy sea and in the dark valley…even into the valley of the shadow of death.

Are you going through a stormy time or a valley experience in your life? The Lord is waiting for you to change your "Why, Lord?" to "I trust You, Lord." The beginning of peace is only a short prayer away.

Dear Lord, thank You for helping our family understand that cancer or other life-shattering trials don't indicate Your disappointment with us. These are my life-shattering events:

_.Continue to help us remember that You are near to those who have a broken heart (see Psalm 34:18).
*Linda Hanna, Indiana

37 Fear Not

Day 30

When thou passest through the waters, I will be with thee; and through the rivers, they shall not overflow thee: when thou walkest through the fire, thou shalt not be burned; neither shall the flame kindle upon thee.
Isaiah 43:2

Where I grew up, the local swimming pool hosted lessons for the children every summer. I was still enough of a beginner that I couldn't yet swim by myself. We were supposed to stay next the edge, holding onto the concrete. The pool ranged from about five to seven feet deep, too deep for eight-year-old girls to be able to walk on the bottom.

On the first day we learned how to hop (pushing ourselves up from the bottom to grab puffs of air at the surface), how to float, and how to kick.

On the second day, we decided we could swim, so my friend and I pushed ourselves away from the edge and paddled. My friend panicked, grabbed me, and we both went under. No one seemed to notice two little girls were in danger. This is when the fear of dying (actually a very good and natural fear to have) kicked in.

Somehow, I convinced her to start hopping, and we did, all the way to the steps. By the time we got there, both of us were gasping and choking and grateful not to have drowned.

Sometimes I wonder how many times God had to rescue me from drowning—not literally in water, but when I took on more than I should have. He lifts me up, over and over again. I remember what happened when Peter, who was walking on the water to Jesus, took his eyes off the Lord and began sinking under the stormy sea: "And immediately Jesus stretched out His hand and caught him...." (NKJV)

Prayer: Lord, Forgive me for allowing pressures to panic me. Help me remember You are bigger than the highest tsunami that can happen in my life. These are my "drowning" fears:

_____

_____

_____. **Thank You that You are there to lift me back to safety when the waters threaten to overflow me. Amen.**

*Anne Baxter Campbell, California

Day 31

"Do not remember the former things, nor consider the things of old. Behold, I will do a new thing, now it shall spring forth; shall you not know it? I will even make a road in the wilderness and rivers in the desert."
Isaiah 43:18-19, NKJV

    It kept appearing before me from a variety of sources. I knew it was from the Lord, but I still didn't know what the new thing was, and I was afraid of what it might be. I like routine. I like to know what's going to happen and when. I've never been a spur-of-the-moment type person. I'm more flexible than I used to be, but I'm still a planner. Stepping out into a new thing is hard. It's scary. There's uncertainty involved. Then I found Isaiah 41:13: "For I, the Lord your God, will hold your right hand, Saying to you, 'Fear not, I will help you.'" (NKJV)

    After I found this verse, God told me what the new thing was—a speaking ministry. I wanted to tell Him that He had the wrong person, like Moses did in Genesis 4. It's not that I don't have things to say, but I'm an introverted introvert (smile). I don't like to be in the limelight. Speakers are front and center. SCARY!

    BUT GOD (I so love those two short words), in His infinite wisdom, made sure I knew He would not send me where He had not prepared me to go. It doesn't mean I am ready to step on stage and speak, but I know He'll be there to help me, to provide the words through the Holy Spirit, if and when I do. It means I'm not doing it alone.

Father, thank You that You are always ready and waiting to help me. I commit my next step of faith to You:

_____

_____

_____

_____. **I will follow wherever You lead, knowing You are preparing the way for me. Amen.**

*Ginger Solomon, Alabama

39 Fear Not

Day 32

And he shall say to them, "Hear, O Israel: Today you are on the verge of battle with your enemies. Do not let your heart faint, do not be afraid, and do not tremble or be terrified because of them; for the Lord your God is He who goes with you, to fight for you against your enemies, to save you." **Deuteronomy 20:3-4, NKJV**

Does fear keep you from moving in the direction God makes clear? Are you inadequate for the job God spreads before you? If so, you are not alone.

For a number of years I prayed for distant friends without hope of ever seeing them. When a door unexpectedly opened to visit them, I rejoiced in God's goodness. As soon as I began preparing for the trip, however, fears and doubt crowded my mind. How could I leave my responsibilities for three weeks? Flying many hours at my age would be too difficult. The expenditure was foolish. How could my visit make any difference?

For forty years, the Israelites looked forward to entering the Promised Land. Jericho was the first large fortified city they faced once they crossed the Jordan. They saw how inadequate they were to take the city. From the world's point of view, a victory was unlikely. Yet most of us have heard the spectacular results of Joshua's obedience.

In today's verses, given to the Israelites before they entered the land, Moses reminds them that taking the land is God's job. He will do the fighting and give the victory if they trust Him and obey. We too will see God's mighty hand working for us if we remember He is the one who fights and wins the victory. We are to trust Him, take the next step He asks of us, and not give in to our fears.

Lord God Almighty, heavenly Father, help us fix our eyes on You instead of on our fears and the defenses of our enemies. You are mighty and loving. Please go before us as we obey You in these things: _____. As we do so, please remind us that we are winning victories for Your glory. Remind us of what You have done, and strengthen our confidence in You. Amen.

*Betsy Baker, Colorado

Day 33

Who shall separate us from the love of Christ? Shall tribulation, or distress, or persecution, or famine, or nakedness, or peril, or sword, Nay, in all these things we are more than conquerors through Him that loved us. For I am persuaded, that neither death, nor life, nor angels, nor principalities, nor powers, nor things present, nor things to come, nor height, nor depth, nor any other creature, shall be able to separate us from the love of God, which is in Christ Jesus our Lord.
Romans 8:35, 37-39

Of all the passages in the Bible, this might be the most comforting. No matter what I go through, He will go through it with me. He will hang onto me. If it's scary, He'll hold my hand. If it's tragic, He'll comfort me. If it's joyful, He laughs with me.

Even when I don't deserve His friendship, He's there for me. Even when I run away from Him, He invites me back. Even when I forget Him, He never, ever forgets me. No matter what I do, where I go, how far I backslide, He's still there. His love is unchanging, undeniable, and eternal—no matter what.

Cling to Him. Jesus will get you through whatever you have to face. And if you need someone to pray for or with you, I will.

Anne Baxter Campbell

E-mail me at anneb1944@aol.com. God bless you.

Prayer: Father God, Holy Spirit, Savior Son, hear my prayer. I come to You sometimes with a broken heart, sometimes terrified of what's happening, sometimes feeling dead from top to toe. This is how I'm feeling now:

_____
_____
_____
_____.

Help me remember, Lord, You are bigger than the mountain, stronger than the tides, and gentler than the softest hug. No matter where I am, You are there. Thank You. Amen and Amen!

A bit about each writer:

Anne Baxter Campbell, a Christian who loves her Lord and her family, is the author of *The Truth Trilogy* and compiler of this devotional. She and her husbandlive in north central California. (Multiple Days)

A retired patent attorney and survivor of advanced breast cancer, *Jan Hasak* wrote two books and maintains a blog, http://janhasak.com/blog/. She plays ukulele and Scrabble and enjoys Bible studies. (Day 1)

Marty Simons is a blogger and internet marketer and has been successfully fighting cancer since 2001. In addition, she is a Christ-Follower, the happy wife of Ross, and also a professional singer and musician. (Day 3)

Eileen Rife is a homeschool mom and author of several fiction and nonfiction titles.
She and her husband conduct marriage seminars and speak on a variety of topics for churches and organizations internationally.
See www.eileenrife.com. (Day 5)

Karen Ingalls is a retired RN, author, and five-plus-year ovarian cancer survivor.
Her book, *Outshine: An Ovarian Cancer Memoir*, is for anyone facing cancer.

All proceeds go to gynecologic cancer research. (Day 7)

Paula Mowery is a pastor's wife, author, and speaker. Her debut novella, *The Blessing Seer*, released in July 2012 from Harbourlight/Pelican Book Group. (Day 9)

Linda Wood Rondeau, author, writes stories filled with poignancy and humor.
Walk with her unforgettable characters as they journey paths not unlike our own. A veteran social worker, the author now resides in Jacksonville, Florida. (Day 11)

Chris Barratt is a freelance writer and homeschool mom who lives in northern Michigan. A graduate of Central Michigan University, she enjoys writing and spending time with her husband and daughters. Contact her at chrisbarrattauthor@gmail.com. (Day 12, Day 21)

Cindy Loven makes her home in Arkansas with her husband and oldest son. She enjoys crafting and reading when she is not thinking up new story ideas for children's books. (Day 14)

David and Joy Rose have been married since March 1996. They have four children and currently live in Minnesota, though their hearts are still with their church family in Willows, CA. (Day 16)

Ralene Burke is a freelance editor and writer who helps people make their work S.H.I.N.E! Outside of writing, she homeschools her three kids and spends time with her adoring husband. (Day 18)

Peggy Blann Phifer is an author of Christian fiction living in northern Wisconsin near her adult children, grandchildren, and great-grandchildren. (Day 20)

Ray N. Hawkins is a retired Churches of Christ Australia minister. He and wife, Mary, have three children and six grandchildren. He has written several devotionals, the latest *Dynamic Aging*. (Day 23)
Email: ray.haw3819@bigpond.com
Blog: http://rayhawkinsauthor.blogspot.com.au

Amy and Alan Disney have been married since 1998 and have two teenaged daughters, Macey and Rylie. Amy is a successful retail manager with a passion for people. (Day 25)

Sue Tornai lives with her husband, John, and dog, Maggie, in Carmichael, California. Many of Sue's devotionals, articles, and stories have been published in magazines and anthologies. (Day 27)

Linda Hanna and her husband, Bill, have been married since 1973. They have three daughters and six grandchildren. Linda is the co-author of a cozy mystery, *Reflections of a Stranger*. (Day 29)

Ginger Solomon is a Christian, a wife, a mother to seven, and a writer—in that order (mostly). Find out more about her at http://gingersolomon.blogspot.com. (Day 32)

Betsy Baker waits expectantly to see God's mighty hand working where she lives in Colorado. (Day 33)

Dedicated to
Patricia "Diann" Hunt
August 2nd 1955 to
November 29th 2013
She wrote:
"I will live this life that God has given me with gusto, not wasting a single moment but using it as He intended. And when my journey here is over, I plan to skid into Glory with a smile on my face, a Bible in one hand, a chocolate truffle in the other, and I will yell at the top of my lungs: Daddy, I'm home."

46 Fear Not